Contents

Nature's powers

What do you think of when someone says 'nature'? Birds, grass and trees? Insects and spiders' webs? Snow, rain, hail and wind? How about lightning, thunderstorms, whirling clouds and raging storms? Baking hot sun? Floods and crashing waves?

Many people imagine gentle things when they think of nature – but the things in the list above are all part of nature. All of them show different kinds of amazing power.

Nature's power can be terrifyingly destructive, like a hurricane or tornado – but the energy behind these storms can also be of great use to humankind.

THE POWER OF NATURE

Becca Heddle

OXFORD
UNIVERSITY PRESS

OXFORD
UNIVERSITY PRESS

Great Clarendon Street, Oxford OX2 6DP

Oxford University Press is a department of the University of Oxford.
It furthers the University's objective of excellence in research, scholarship,
and education by publishing worldwide in

Oxford   New York

Auckland   Cape Town   Dar es Salaam   Hong Kong   Karachi
Kuala Lumpur   Madrid   Melbourne   Mexico City   Nairobi
New Delhi   Shanghai   Taipei   Toronto

With offices in

Argentina   Austria   Brazil   Chile   Czech Republic   France   Greece
Guatemala   Hungary   Italy   Japan   Poland   Portugal   Singapore
South Korea   Switzerland   Thailand   Turkey   Ukraine   Vietnam

Oxford is a registered trade mark of Oxford University Press
in the UK and in certain other countries

Text © Becca Heddle 2005

The moral rights of the author have been asserted

Database right Oxford University Press (maker)

First published 2005

British Library Cataloguing in Publication Data

Data available

ISBN 978-0-19-919884-9

17 19 20 18 16

Printed in China by Imago

Acknowledgements

The publisher would like to thank the following for permission to reproduce
photographs: **Title page** OUP; **p3** OUP; **p4**t photolibrary.com/Faidley Warren, b Corbis; **p5**t
Science Photo Library/PLI, b Corbis/Jose Luis Pelaez Inc; **p7**t Science Photo Library/Mehau Kulyk,
b Alamy/Gianni Muratore; **p8** Corbis/Kevin R Morris; **p9** Corbis/Mark A Johnson; **p10** Corbis/Layne
Kennedy; **p11**t Alamy/Janine Weidel, b Hagbourne School; **p12** Science Photo Library/Adam Hart-
Davis; **p13**t Still Pictures/Mark Edwards, b Corbis/Jean Becker/Sygma; **p14** Alamy/A T Willett; **p15**
NASA; **p20/21**t Corbis/Kerstin Geier; **p20** MEN Syndidcation; **p21** Corbis/Owaki-Kulla; **p22**t OUP,
b Alamy/S T Yapp; **p24**t Corbis, b Alamy/Robert Harding Picture Library; **p25**t Alamy/Apex News &
Picture Agency, b Corbis/Lana Slivar/Reuters; **p26**t Corbis/Hubert Stadler, b Alamy/Keren Su; **p27**
Alamy/Worldwide Picture Library, b Corbis/Wild Country; **p28**t Corbis/Robert Whistler/Cordaiy
Picture Library, b Alamy/Photofusion Picture Library; **p29** Ecoscene/Photographers Direct; **p30**t
Corbis/Joel W Rogers, b Corbis/Craig Lovell

Cover photograph by Corbis/William James Warren

The author would like to thank Guy Ottewell for his kind permission to use his solar system
model 'The thousand-yard model: the Earth as a peppercorn': www.universalworkshop.com

Illustrations by Stefan Chabluk; **p6, p9, p10, p14, p15, p16, p17, p19**b, **p23, p29**;
Sean Longcroft; **p8, p12, p18, p19**t

Special thanks to Richard Jones of Hagbourne C. E. School

As more of the world's countries develop and need to use more energy, the **resources** on which **industrialised countries** depend are running out. We need to make the most of these resources, and also to avoid worsening the problems of pollution and **climate change** which we have already set in motion. This means using wisely the vast power that nature provides.

This book is about discovering the astonishing power that can be sourced from the Sun's heat and light, from the wind and from water. Find out about ways that this power can be – and is being – harnessed to provide energy to help humans live in safety and comfort.

All about the Sun

Did you know that the Sun is a star? It looks much brighter than all the other stars because it is very much closer to us. It is 150 million kilometres away – and the Earth would fit inside it more than a million times.

Here's a way to get an idea of this **scale**.

You will need:

- a peppercorn
  (to represent the Earth)
- a football
  (to represent the Sun)
- a football field
- a friend

Ask your friend to hold a peppercorn at one end of the football field.

Take the football and run down the pitch, stopping about a quarter of the way down the field (about 26 metres).

If the Earth was the size of a peppercorn, this is how far it would be from the Sun.

This is the size relationship between the Earth (the peppercorn) and the Sun (the football).

But what is a star? A star is a ball of very hot gas. It shines because it is making massive amounts of energy deep inside.

This energy process uses vast amounts of raw materials. Every second the Sun loses about 4 million tonnes of mass which it cannot replace. But it has been working at this rate for nearly 5 **billion** years, and can last several billion more.

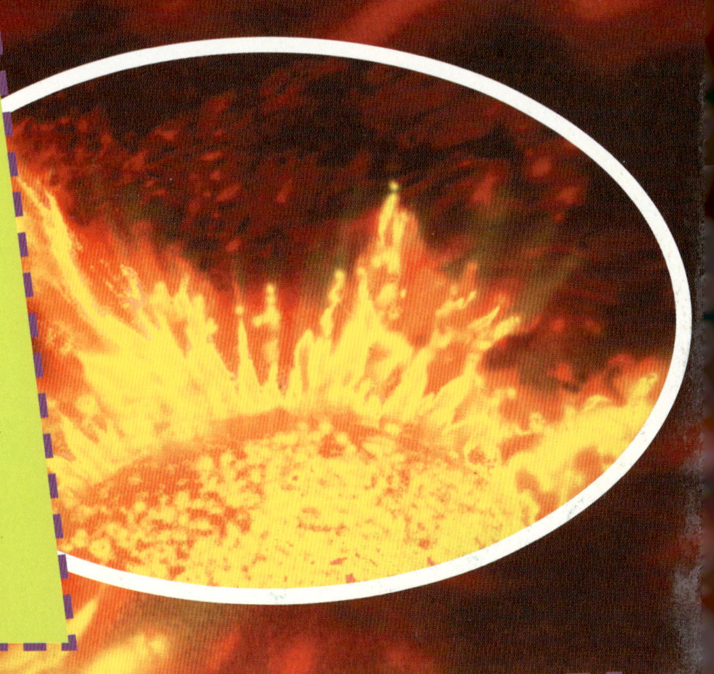

The Sun makes a terrifying amount of heat. Its surface temperature is estimated at about 5700 degrees Celsius – remember, water boils at 100 degrees Celsius. The Sun's centre is even hotter: about 15 million degrees Celsius. No wonder the Sun's heat can burn your skin, even though that heat has travelled millions of kilometres to reach you.

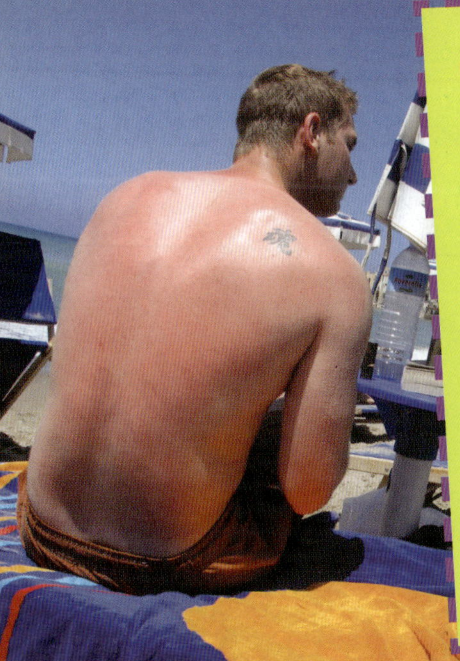

All done by the Sun

The Sun makes all the light we see on Earth, apart from the stars' twinkling. Even moonlight is actually reflected sunlight – the Moon doesn't make any light of its own. The Sun's light and energy take only about 8 minutes to come the 150 million kilometres to us.

The Sun's light and heat warm up the surface of the Earth and our **atmosphere**. Heating air makes the air move – hold a piece of tissue paper over a warm radiator and you will see how the warm air rises. In the same way, currents of warm air rise up through the atmosphere when the sun warms the Earth's surface.

As the air rises, it gets cooler, so it sinks again. The effect of the sun's heat sets up huge currents of rising and falling air in the atmosphere. We feel moving air as winds. As the Earth turns, the air currents are dragged along – so winds blow around the Earth, instead of just north and south.

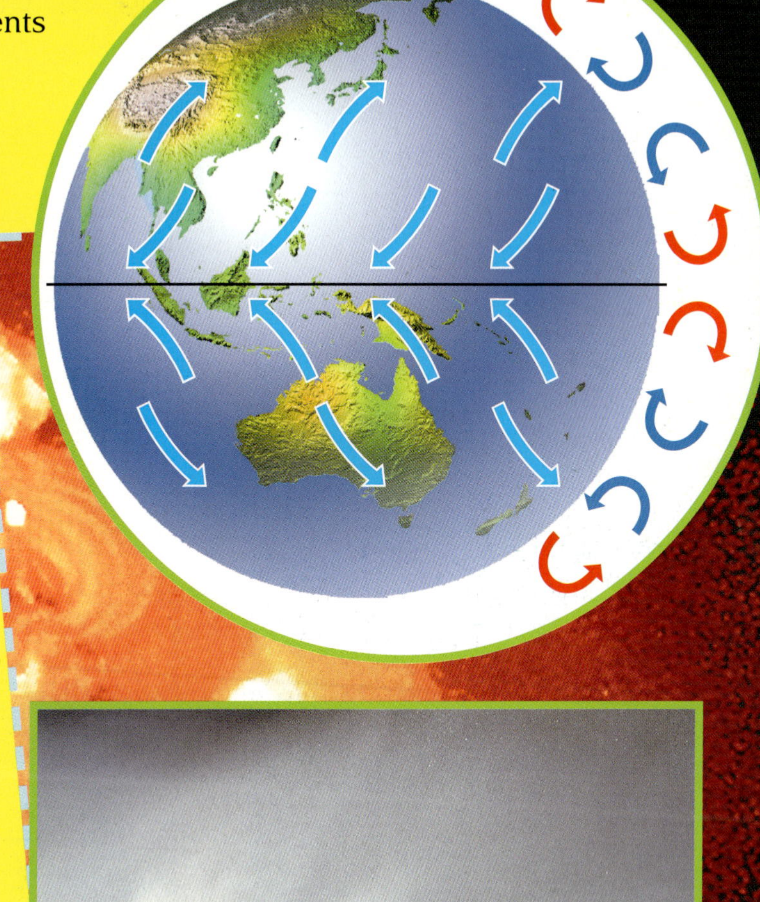

When wind blows over the sea (or any large body of water) it causes waves. The power of the waves is another important kind of energy. See pages 28 to 29 for more information about waves.

While the Sun is the basis of every kind of natural power on Earth, we can also use its power in more direct ways, too. The next few pages are about ways we use the Sun's light and heat.

Using the Sun's heat

☼ People on safari holidays in hot countries often use a 'solar shower' like this. It uses the heat of the Sun to warm the water.

On a warm, sunny day, you can do something similar at home.

- Find a large plastic tub or a paddling pool, and stand it outside, where it will be in the sun most of the day.

- Put a big dark bag in it, like a plastic rubbish bag, and pour cold water into the bag. Fold the top over.

- Leave the bag in the sun all day if possible, then open it. The water is warm, because heat from the Sun has been absorbed by the dark bag and **conducted** to the water.

- To see how much the Sun has heated the water in the bag, turn on a cold tap and feel the difference in temperature between the two.

Only fill it a few centimetres deep.

Some houses use devices called solar collectors to heat up water for washing and baths, and even for central heating. The devices collect the Sun's heat and conduct it to water. In a hot country, they can provide most of a house's hot water, even on overcast days. In Greece, most houses and some hotels have solar collectors on their roofs.

This primary school in Oxfordshire, in the United Kingdom, uses solar matting to heat its swimming pool.

Using the power of light

☼ As well as using the Sun's power to heat water, we can make electricity directly from its light.

☼ Have you or someone you know got a calculator like this? The little panels by the display are solar cells, also called photovoltaic cells (say *photo-volt-**ay**-ick*). The metals inside them convert light directly into electricity.

It takes very little light to power the calculator.

☼ You can prove that the light is powering the calculator. Just cover up the cells one by one, with the calculator switched on. When you have blocked out most of the light, the numbers on the display go dim, and then disappear.

A solar panel is made up of a number of solar cells. People all over the world use solar panels on their roofs or walls to provide their homes with electricity. They are also used to power weather stations, and you can see telephone boxes with solar panels in places where there is no **mains electricity**.

This school in India uses solar panels to power electrical equipment.

The Breitling Orbiter, the first balloon to fly round the world, used photovoltaic power to run its navigation and communication equipment.

> Tornadoes and hurricanes are two different kinds of powerful, dangerous wind storms.

> Tornadoes are related to thunderstorms. The strong air currents inside a storm cloud can create a funnel of wind: at the centre, the winds can whip round at more than 480 kilometres per hour. If the funnel reaches down to the ground, it can cause terrible destruction. It can suck up things from the ground, including animals, cars, houses – and even people.

> This part of the USA is known as 'tornado alley'. People have storm cellars to hide in when tornadoes come, because their houses may become completely flattened.

➤ Hurricanes are caused by air moving over warm tropical sea. The warmth of the water heats the air, which rises very quickly in a column.

➤ At the surface of the sea, cool air rushes in to replace the warm air. This cool air then heats up, and spirals upwards too.

➤ This circular process continues and the air moves more and more strongly.

➤ A hurricane loses its power when it moves over land. Land provides less warmth to heat the rising air, and slows down the hurricane.

➤ Hurricanes are also called typhoons and tropical cyclones, depending on exactly where they strike.

This satellite image shows deadly Typhoon Winnie over the Philippines in October 2004.

Measuring wind

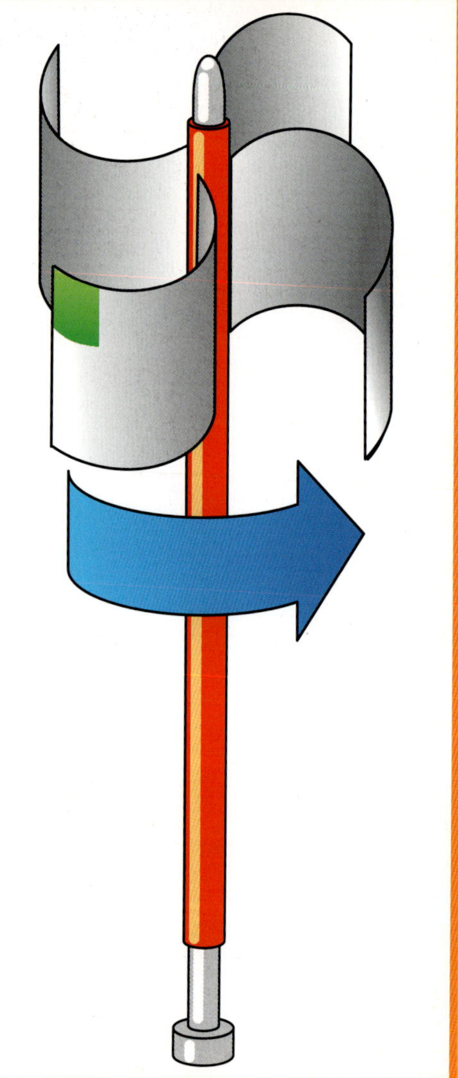

- Try making this simple wind measure, called an anemometer (say *an-em-**om**-eter*), to get an idea of how fast wind can blow.

  You will need:
  - a straw
  - a knitting needle
  - a cardboard tube
  - sticky tape
  - a coloured pen

- Cut the cardboard tube in half both lengthways and widthways.

- Tape the pieces to the straw, so they make a windmill shape.

- Slide the straw over the knitting needle.

- Colour in a corner of one of the pieces of cardboard. Now blow – or better still, take the anemometer out in the wind.

- How fast does it turn? Can you count the number of times the coloured square goes past in a minute?

➤ Unless there is almost no wind, the anemometer moves so fast it is impossible to count. That is why in 1805 Admiral Sir Francis Beaufort thought up a way of measuring the strength of wind, based on what you can see it doing. His original version was based on weather at sea, but the Beaufort Scale has been adapted for land.

Force 1:
1–5 kph

Force 7:
50–61 kph

Force 2:
6–11 kph

Force 8:
62–74 kph

Force 3:
12–19 kph

Force 9:
75–88 kph

Force 4:
20–28 kph

Force 10:
89–102 kph

Force 5:
29–38 kph

Force 11:
103–117 kph

Force 6:
39–49 kph

Force 12:
over 117 kph

kph = kilometres per hour

Using the wind

Try this experiment to see how easy it is to use the wind's power.

You will need:

- cardboard
- scissors
- string
- a straw
- thread
- sticky tape
- a knitting needle
- a paper clip or other light weight

- Draw round a plate or bowl on the cardboard.

- Cut out the circle of card, then put a glass roughly in the middle and draw round that.

- Snip four cuts into the circle of card, each just up to the inner circle.

- Fold over the four edges, like this.

- Make a hole in the middle with a pen, then slide the windmill onto a straw. Tape it on if it's wobbly.

- Slide the straw over a knitting needle, and blow to test your windmill.

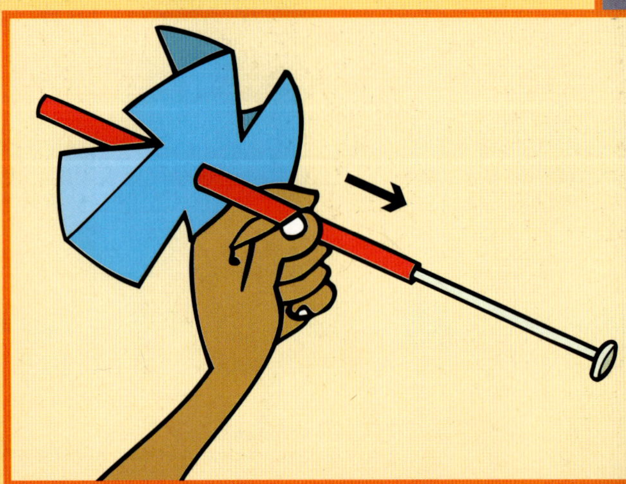

● Tie a piece of thread about 30 cm long to your weight, and tape the other end to the straw.

● Now blow again – watch the weight wind up!

➤ You have made a very simple windmill – it doesn't pull very hard because your breath has only a tiny fraction of the real wind's power. But people all over the world use big versions of windmills like this to draw water up from wells, run **irrigation systems** and even make electricity.

Wind farms: for and against

Against wind farms

Wind farms are industrial complexes – they should be called wind factories. They are enormous, ugly, and noisy – each turbine makes as much noise as a motorbike. They spoil the view and would ruin the countryside.

The turbines kill birds which fly into the blades.

They don't even generate much electricity! They only work when the wind is blowing, and when it isn't, other sources of power are needed to make up the difference.

For wind farms

8 out of 10 people say they are in favour of wind farms – especially people who actually live near one – so they can't be that ugly and noisy.

No more birds are killed by wind turbines than by cars and power lines. Besides, the ground around a wind farm could not be built on, so it would be ideal for birds to nest in.

Wind farms could be built in the sea too. Because there is so much sea around Britain, offshore wind power could meet twice the UK's total energy needs.

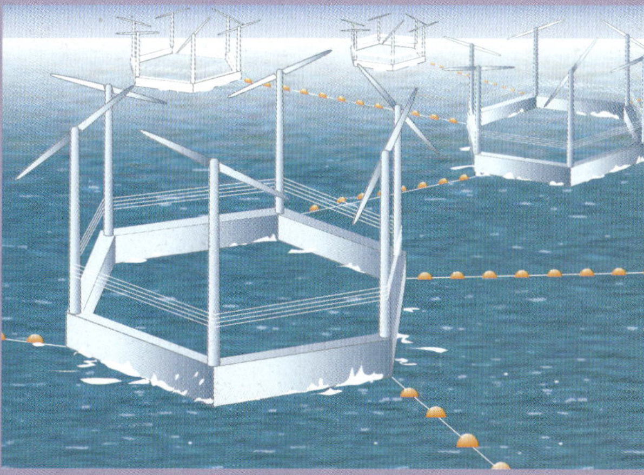

Always moving

Have you ever seen water lying completely still? Even the smooth surface of a glass of water moves if you touch the glass.

Now think about water in nature: streams are constantly flowing; there are always waves or ripples on lakes and in the sea. And then there are tides, whirlpools and waterfalls…

Water is in the air, even when you can't see it. You see the clouds in the sky, and the rain and snow that can fall from them – but you can't see the water getting up into the clouds in the first place. It is all part of a great cycle, driven by the power of the Sun.

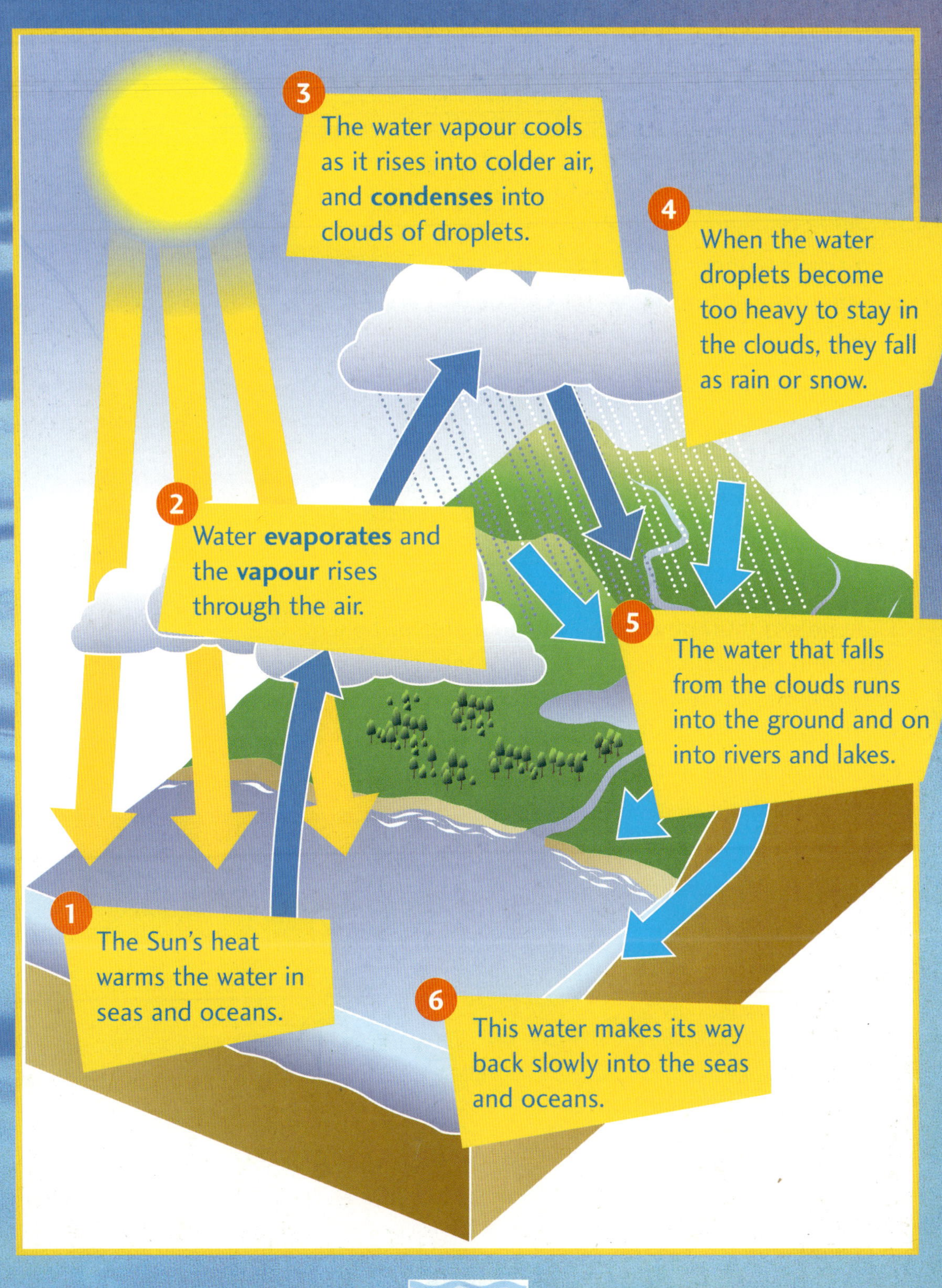

3 The water vapour cools as it rises into colder air, and condenses into clouds of droplets.
4 When the water droplets become too heavy to stay in the clouds, they fall as rain or snow.
2 Water evaporates and the vapour rises through the air.
5 The water that falls from the clouds runs into the ground and on into rivers and lakes.
1 The Sun's heat warms the water in seas and oceans.
6 This water makes its way back slowly into the seas and oceans.

Water: life and death

Water is possibly the most important thing involved in keeping us alive. A person can survive for weeks without food, but only for a few days without water. But while a drink of water is vital for life, water can be a powerful and dangerous thing too.

Have you ever watched a waterfall swirling down a mountainside or seen the sea crashing over rocks? Then you have seen something of the power of water.

The endless thumping of waves on a cliff or beach can grind the hugest boulders down into smooth pebbles, and eventually into sand. This hotel in Scarborough crumbled into the sea because waves **eroded** the cliff it was built on.

In some countries, people struggle to get enough water for their daily lives. The ground can be parched and cracked, rock hard and impossible to plant crops in. This means that when rain does come, it runs straight over without soaking in. Heavy rainstorms can cause terrible damage to houses, crops and lives – even in countries like Britain.

This flood in Devon in 2004 swept cars out to sea and ruined homes and businesses.

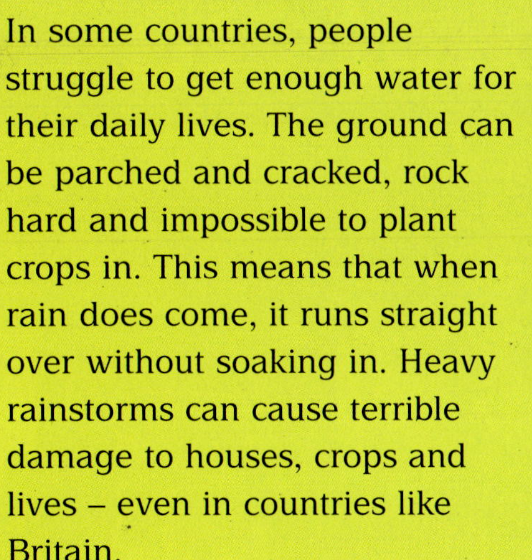

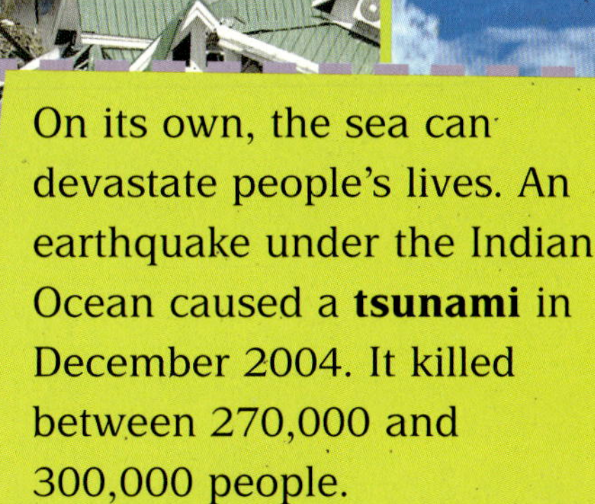

On its own, the sea can devastate people's lives. An earthquake under the Indian Ocean caused a **tsunami** in December 2004. It killed between 270,000 and 300,000 people.

From millponds to mountains

People have used the power of water for many thousands of years, starting with simple water wheels. They work like windmills, but they are turned by the constant movement of a stream or river.

Now people build dams to make **reservoirs** and attach power stations to them. When the water behind the dam is released, it turns huge turbines which make electricity.

You can see dams like these all over the world: the biggest one planned is the Chinese Three Gorges dam. It should be completed in 2009, and provide one-ninth of all China's power needs.

Vast dams like this are controversial – building the reservoirs causes widespread destruction, and may increase the risk of earthquakes.

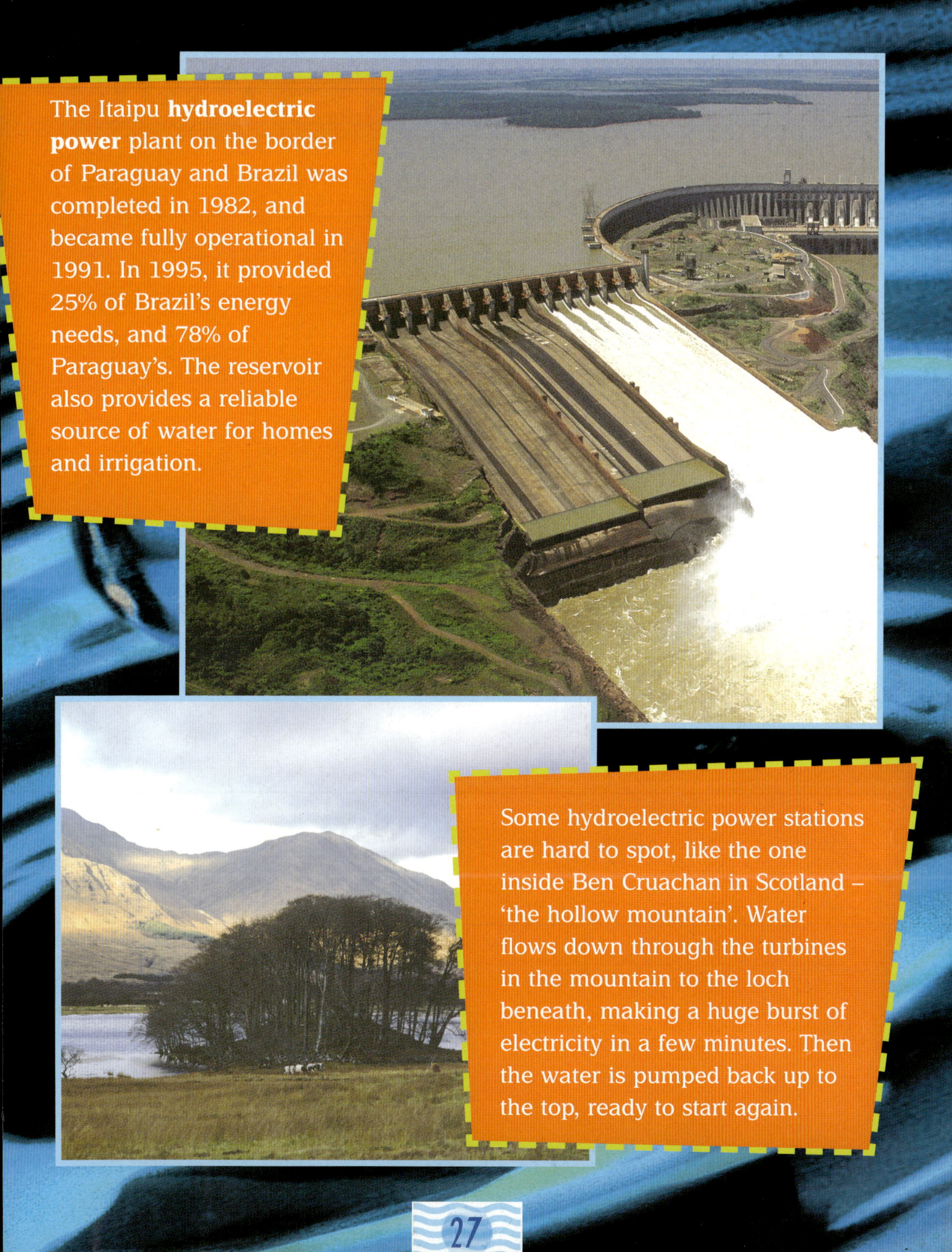

The Itaipu **hydroelectric power** plant on the border of Paraguay and Brazil was completed in 1982, and became fully operational in 1991. In 1995, it provided 25% of Brazil's energy needs, and 78% of Paraguay's. The reservoir also provides a reliable source of water for homes and irrigation.

Some hydroelectric power stations are hard to spot, like the one inside Ben Cruachan in Scotland – 'the hollow mountain'. Water flows down through the turbines in the mountain to the loch beneath, making a huge burst of electricity in a few minutes. Then the water is pumped back up to the top, ready to start again.

Using the sea's power

The sea is constantly moving, in two main ways. The first is in waves, caused by wind and currents.

The other way the sea moves is with the tides. Because of the way the Moon's **gravity** pulls at the water, all seas have two high tides and two low tides in every 24 hours.

Both waves and tides can be used to make power.

One of the most popular sites so far for making **tidal** power is river estuaries: the part of rivers that feed into the sea and are tidal. This dam on the River Rance in France makes enough energy to supply 300,000 people with power.

New projects are constantly opening up the possibility of wave-motion power. This machine, which was installed on the Scottish island of Islay in 2000, is called the Limpet – Land Installed **Marine** Power Energy Transformer. Waves go into it and compress air, which flows through turbines to make electricity, and just this one machine provides power for about 400 homes.

The **prototype** of another project, the Pelamis 'snake' was trialled in the Orkney islands in 2004. It wiggles with the waves, and transmits the energy back along cables to the shore. A Pelamis 'wave farm' one kilometre square could provide electricity for over 20,000 homes.

There's always more

The kinds of energy in this book are available all over the world. Unlike coal, oil or gas, they will never run out in the Earth's lifetime.

Many scientists now agree that the Earth's climate is being affected by humankind burning so much oil, coal and gas. The gases given off are making the world warmer. Some scientists say this is increasing the dangers of nature, with droughts, hurricanes and floods becoming more frequent than before.

But if we start making the most of nature's fantastic powers, this could help to slow down or even reverse this change, for the good of all the people in the world.

Glossary

atmosphere – the layer of gases surrounding the Earth

billion – a thousand million

climate change – the gases made by humankind burning oil, coal and gas are making the Earth get warmer

condense – to turn from a vapour (like steam) into a liquid (like water)

conduct – if something conducts heat, it passes heat to another material which it is touching

erode – wear away

evaporate – to turn from a liquid (like water) into a vapour (like steam)

gravity – the force that keeps things on the ground and that makes things fall

hydroelectric power – power made by water turning turbines

industrialised countries – countries in the developed world which use lots of energy

irrigation systems – networks of channels to direct water to crops

mains electricity – electricity from a national energy system, which comes into the home through wires

marine – of the sea

prototype – a trial model of a machine

reservoir – lake made by damming rivers

resources – raw materials

scale – the relative sizes of things

tidal – made by the tides, or rising and falling with them

tsunami – a huge wave, caused by an earthquake or volcanic eruption

vapour – minute droplets of liquid found in the air (like steam)

Index